# Head

MW00489630

LEISURE ARTS, INC. • Little Rock, Arkansas

# DAISY DELIGHT

 **EASY**

## SHOPPING LIST

**Yarn** (Medium Weight)
[7 ounces, 364 yards
(198 grams, 333 meters) per skein]:

☐ Green - One skein
☐ White - 10 yards (9 meters)
☐ Yellow - small amount

### Crochet Hook

☐ Size H (5 mm)
   **or** size needed for gauge

### Additional Supplies

☐ Yarn needle

## SIZE INFORMATION

**Approximate Finished
Measurement (excluding tie)**

Girl's   3¼" wide x 14" long
         (8.5 cm x 35.5 cm)

Teen's   4½" wide x 17" long
         (11.5 cm x 43 cm)

*Size Note:* We have printed the instructions for the sizes in different colors to make it easier for you to find:

• Girl's size in Blue
• Teen's size in Pink

Instructions in Black apply to both sizes.

## GAUGE INFORMATION

In pattern, (Cluster, ch 2, Cluster, ch 1) 4 times = 4½" (11.5 cm)
**Gauge Swatch:** 4" (10 cm) square
With Green, ch 17.
**Row 1:** Dc in fourth ch from hook and in each ch across: 15 sts.
**Rows 2-6:** Ch 3 (**counts as first dc**), turn; dc in next dc and in each st across.
Finish off.

## ─── STITCH GUIDE ───

**CLUSTER** (uses one st)

★ YO, insert hook in st indicated, YO and pull up a loop, YO and draw through 2 loops on hook; repeat from ★ once **more**, YO and draw through all 3 loops on hook.

**SINGLE CROCHET 2 TOGETHER**
   *(abbreviated sc2tog)*

Pull up a loop in each of next 2 sts, YO and draw through all 3 loops on hook (**counts as one sc**).

# INSTRUCTIONS
## BODY

With Green, ch 44{52}.

**Row 1** (Right side)**:** Working in back ridges of beginning ch *(Fig. 1, page 46)*, sc in second ch from hook and in next 2 chs, ch 1, skip next ch, (hdc in next 3 chs, ch 1, skip next ch) 3 times, (dc in next 3 chs, ch 1, skip next ch) 3{5} times, (hdc in next 3 chs, ch 1, skip next ch) 3 times, sc in last 3 chs: 33{39} sts and 10{12} chs.

*Note:* Loop a short piece of yarn around any stitch to mark Row 1 as **right** side.

**Row 2:** Ch 1, turn; sc in first 3 sc, ch 1, skip next ch and next hdc, work (Cluster, ch 2, Cluster) in next hdc, ch 1, ★ skip next 3 sts, work (Cluster, ch 2, Cluster) in next st, ch 1 repeat from ★ 7{9} times **more**, skip next hdc and next ch, sc in last 3 sc: 9{11} ch-2 sps.

**Row 3:** Ch 1, turn; sc in first 3 sc, ch 1 skip next ch and next Cluster, (3 hdc in next ch-2 sp, ch 1, skip next 3 sts) times, (3 dc in next ch-2 sp, ch 1, skip next 3 sts) 3{5} times, (3 hdc in next ch-2 sp, ch 1, skip next 3 sts) twice, 3 hdc in next ch-2 sp, ch 1, skip next Cluster and next ch, sc in last 3 sc: 43{51} sts.

**Rows 4 thru 5{7}:** Repeat Rows 2 and 3, 1{2} time(s).

Do **not** finish off.

## FIRST TIE END

**Row 1:** Ch 1, do **not** turn; working in end of rows, work 5{6} sc evenly spaced across: 5{6} sc.

**Row 2:** Ch 1, turn; skip first sc, sc in last 4{5} sc: 4{5} sc.

**Row 3:** Ch 1, turn; skip first sc, sc in last 3{4} sc: 3{4} sc.

**Teen's Size ONLY**

**Row 4:** Ch 1, turn; skip first sc, sc in last 3 sc: 3 sc.

**Both Sizes**

**Last Row:** Ch 1, turn; skip first sc, sc2tog, ch 16 for tie; finish off.

## SECOND TIE END

**Row 1:** With **right** side facing and working in ends of rows across opposite end of Body, join Green with sc in first row *(see Joining With Sc, page 46)*; work 4{5} sc evenly spaced across: 5{6} sc.

Complete same as First Tie End.

## FLOWER

**Rnd 1** (Right side)**:** With Yellow, ch 2; 8 sc in second ch from hook; join with slip st to first sc.

*Note:* Mark Rnd 1 as **right** side.

**Rnd 2:** Ch 1, 2 sc in same st and in each sc around; join with slip st to first sc, finish off: 16 sc.

**Rnd 3:** With **right** side facing, join White with sc in any sc; ch 12, slip st in same st, (sc, ch 12, slip st) in next sc and in each sc around; join with slip st to first sc, finish off.

Using photo as a guide for placement, sew Flower to Body.

# SIMPLY ELEGANT

 **EASY**

## SIZE INFORMATION

**Approximate Finished
Measurement (excluding tie)**

Girl's    4" wide x 14½" long
          (10 cm x 37 cm)

Teen's    4" wide x 15½" long
          (10 cm x 39.5 cm)

*Size Note:* We have printed the instructions for the sizes in different colors to make it easier for you to find:

• Girl's size in Blue
• Teen's size in Pink

Instructions in Black apply to both sizes.

## GAUGE INFORMATION
**GAUGE SWATCH:**
   2½" (6.25 cm) diameter
Work same as Flower, page 8, through Rnd 2; do **not** finish off.

## INSTRUCTIONS
### BODY
**Row 1:** Ch 21 (tie made); hdc in third ch from hook, leave remaining chs unworked: one hdc.

**Row 2** (Right side)**:** Ch 1, turn; sc in first hdc: one sc.

Place a short piece of yarn in first sc for st placement.

**Row 3:** Ch 46{50}, sc in second ch from hook and in next ch: 2 sc.

**Row 4:** Ch 42{46}; with **right** side facing and being careful **not** to twist chs, slip st in sc on Row 2.

**Row 5:** Ch 42{46}; with **wrong** side facing and being careful **not** to twist chs, slip st in next 2 sc on Row 3, ch 18 for tie; finish off.

## FLOWER

**Rnd 1** (Right side)**:** Ch 2, 12 sc in second ch from hook; do **not** join, place a marker to mark the beginning of the rnd *(see Markers, page 45).*

*Note:* Loop a short piece of yarn around any stitch to mark Rnd 1 as **right** side.

**Rnd 2:** Sc in next sc, (ch 3, sc in next sc) around, ch 1, hdc in next sc to form last ch-3 sp: 12 ch-3 sps.

**Rnd 3:** Ch 3, (sc in next ch-3 sp, ch 3) around; join with slip st to first ch of beginning ch-3.

**Rnd 4:** Ch 1, (sc, dc, ch 1, dc, sc) in each ch-3 sp around; join with slip st to first sc, finish off.

Using photo as a guide for placement, sew Flower to Body.

# SO REFINED

Shown on page 11.

◀■■☐☐ **EASY**

## SHOPPING LIST

**Yarn** (Medium Weight)
[7 ounces, 364 yards
(198 grams, 333 meters) per skein]:
☐ One skein

### Crochet Hook
☐ Size I (5.5 mm)
   **or** size needed for gauge

### Additional Supplies
☐ Yarn needle
☐ Sewing needle and thread
☐ ¾" (19 mm) Button

## SIZE INFORMATION

**Approximate Finished
Measurement (excluding tie)**

Girl's    4½" wide x 16" long
          (11.5 cm x 40.5 cm)
Teen's    4½" wide x 19" long
          (11.5 cm x 48.5 cm)

*Size Note:* We have printed the instructions for the sizes in different colors to make it easier for you to find:
• Girl's size in Blue
• Teen's size in Pink
Instructions in Black apply to both sizes.

## GAUGE INFORMATION

In pattern, (Cluster, ch 2, Cluster) 4
   times = 4½" (11.5 cm)
**Gauge Swatch:** 4" (10 cm) square
Ch 17.
**Row 1:** Sc in second ch from hook
and in each ch across: 16 sc.
**Rows 2-16:** Ch 1, turn; sc in each sc
across.
Finish off.

**CLUSTER** (uses one st)

★ YO, insert hook in st indicated, YO and pull up a loop, YO and draw through 2 loops on hook; repeat from ★ 2 times **more**, YO and draw through all 4 loops on hook.

## INSTRUCTIONS
### BODY

Ch 41{50}.

**Row 1:** Working in back ridges of beginning ch *(Fig. 1, page 46)*, sc in second ch from hook and in next 5 chs, hdc in next 9{12} chs, dc in next 10{13} chs, hdc in next 9{12} chs, sc in last 6 chs: 40{49} sts.

**Row 2** (Right side)**:** Ch 1, turn; sc in first 5 sc, skip next sc, work (Cluster, ch 2, Cluster) in next hdc, ★ skip next 2 sts, work (Cluster, ch 2, Cluster) in next st; repeat from ★ 8{11} times **more**, skip next sc, sc in last 5 sc: 30{36} sts and 10{13} ch-2 sps.

*Note:* Loop a short piece of yarn around any stitch to mark Row 2 as **right** side.

**Row 3:** Ch 1, turn; sc in first 5 sc, ch 1, [skip next Cluster, 2 hdc in next ch-2 sp, hdc in sp **between** next 2 Clusters *(Fig. 4, page 46)*] 3{4} times, skip next Cluster, 2 dc in next ch-2 sp, [dc in sp **between** next 2 Clusters, skip next Cluster, 2 dc in next ch-2 sp] 3{4} times, [hdc in sp **between** next 2 Clusters, skip next Cluster, 2 hdc in next ch-2 sp] 3{4} times, ch 1, skip next Cluster, sc in last 5 sc: 41{50} sts.

**Row 4:** Ch 1, turn; sc in first 5 sc, skip next ch, hdc in next hdc, skip next hdc, work (Cluster, ch 2, Cluster) in next hdc, ★ skip next 2 sts, work (Cluster, ch 2, Cluster) in next st; repeat from ★ 7{10} times **more**, skip next hdc, hdc in next hdc, skip next ch, sc in last 5 sc: 30{36} sts and 9{12} ch-2 sps.

**Row 5:** Ch 1, turn; sc in first 5 sc, ch 1, hdc in next hdc, skip next Cluster, 2 hdc in next ch-2 sp, [hdc in sp **between** next 2 Clusters, skip next Cluster, 2 hdc in next ch-2 sp] 2{3} times, dc in sp **between** next 2 Clusters, [skip next Cluster, 2 dc in next ch-2 sp, dc in sp **between** next 2 Clusters] 3{4} times, skip next Cluster, 2 hdc in next ch-2 sp, [hdc in sp **between** next 2 Clusters, skip next Cluster, 2 hdc in next ch-2 sp] 2{3} times, skip next Cluster, hdc in next hdc, ch 1, sc in last 5 sc: 40{49} sts.

**Row 6:** Ch 1, turn; sc in first 5 sc, skip next ch, work (Cluster, ch 2, Cluster) in next hdc, ★ skip next 2 sts, work (Cluster, ch 2, Cluster) in next st; repeat from ★ 8{11} times **more**, skip next ch, sc in last 5 sc: 30{36} sts and 10{13} ch-2 sps.

**Row 7:** Ch 1, turn; sc in first 5 sc, [skip next Cluster, 2 hdc in next ch-2 sp, hdc in sp **between** next 2 Clusters] 3{4} times, skip next Cluster, 2 dc in next ch-2 sp, [dc in sp **between** next 2 Clusters, skip next Cluster, 2 dc in next ch-2 sp] 3{4} times, [hdc in sp **between** next 2 Clusters, skip next Cluster, 2 hdc in next ch-2 sp] 3{4} times, skip next Cluster, sc in last 5 sc; do **not** finish off.

**BUTTON END**

**Row 1:** Ch 1, do **not** turn; working in end of rows, work 5 sc evenly spaced across.

**Row 2:** Ch 1, turn; skip first sc, sc in next 3 sc, slip st in last sc: 3 sc.

**Row 3:** Ch 1, turn; skip first slip st, sc in next 2 sc, slip st in last sc; finish off.

## BUTTONHOLE END

**Row 1:** With **wrong** side facing and working in end of rows across opposite end of Body, join yarn with sc in first row *(see Joining With Sc, page 46)*; sc in next row, ch 2 (buttonhole), skip next 3 rows, sc in last 2 rows: 4 sc and one ch-2 sp.

**Row 2:** Ch 1, turn; skip first sc, sc in next sc and in next ch-2 sp, sc in next sc, slip st in last sc: 3 sc.

**Row 3:** Ch 1, turn; skip first slip st, sc in next 2 sc, slip st in last sc; finish off.

Sew button to Button End.

## FLOWER

Ch 4; join with slip st to form a ring.

**Rnd 1** (Right side)**:** Ch 5 (**counts as first dc plus ch 2**), (2 dc in ring, ch 2) 5 times, dc in ring; join with slip st to first dc: 6 ch-2 sps.

*Note:* Mark Rnd 1 as **right** side.

**Rnd 2:** Ch 1, (sc, 5 dc, sc) in first ch-2 sp and in each ch-2 sp around; join with slip st to first sc, finish off.

Using photo as a guide for placement, sew Flower to Body.

# PETAL POWER

 **EASY**

## SHOPPING LIST

### Yarn (Medium Weight)

[6 ounces, 315 yards
(170 grams, 288 meters) per skein]:

- ☐ Lavender - One skein
- ☐ Purple - 15 yards (13.5 meters)
- ☐ Variegated - Small amount

### Crochet Hook

- ☐ Size H (5 mm)

  **or** size needed for gauge

### Additional Supplies

- ☐ Yarn needle

## SIZE INFORMATION

**Approximate Finished
Measurement (excluding tie)**

Girl's      3½" wide x 19" long
            (9 cm x 48.5 cm)

Teen's     4½" wide x 21½" long
            (11.5 cm x 54.5 cm)

*Size Note:* We have printed the instructions for the sizes in different colors to make it easier for you to find:

- Girl's size in Blue
- Teen's size in Pink

Instructions in Black apply to both sizes.

## GAUGE INFORMATION

In pattern, 14 sts = 4" (10 cm)

**Gauge Swatch:** 4" wide x 3½" high
    (10 cm x 9 cm)

With Purple, ch 16.

**Row 1:** Dc in fourth ch from hook
**(3 skipped chs count as first dc)** and in each ch across: 14 dc.

**Rows 2-7:** Ch 3 **(counts as first dc)**, turn; dc in next dc and in each dc across.

Finish off.

# INSTRUCTIONS
## BODY

With Lavender, ch 47{55}.

**Row 1** (Right side)**:** Working in back ridges of beginning ch *(Fig. 1, page 46)*, sc in second ch from hook and in next 7 chs, hdc in next 11{13} chs, dc in next 8{12} chs, hdc in next 11{13} chs, sc in last 8 chs: 46{54} sts.

*Note:* Loop a short piece of yarn around any stitch to mark Row 1 as **right** side.

**Row 2:** Ch 1, turn; sc in first 8 sc, ★ skip next st, dc in next st, working **behind** last dc made, dc in skipped st (**Cross St made**); repeat from ★ across to last 8 sc, sc in last 8 sc: 16 sc and 15{19} Cross Sts.

**Row 3:** Ch 1, turn; sc in first 8 sc, hdc in next 11{13} dc, dc in next 8{12} dc, hdc in next 11{13} dc, sc in last 8 sc: 46{54} sts.

**Rows 4 thru 7{9}:** Repeat Rows 2 and 3, 2{3} times.

Do **not** finish off.

## FIRST TIE END

**Row 1:** Ch 2, do **not** turn; work 5{7} dc evenly spaced across end of rows: 5{7} dc.

**Row 2:** Ch 2, turn; skip first dc, dc in last 4{6} dc: 4{6} dc.

**Row 3:** Ch 2, turn; skip first dc, dc in last 3{5} dc: 3{5} dc.

**Row 4:** Ch 2, turn; skip first dc, dc in last 2{4} dc: 2{4} dc.

**Teen's Size ONLY**
**Row 5:** Ch 2, turn; skip first dc, dc in last 3 dc: 3 dc.

**Row 6:** Ch 2, turn; skip first dc, dc in last 2 dc: 2 dc.

**Both Sizes**

**Last Row:** Ch 2, turn; skip first dc, dc in last dc, ch 16 for tie; finish off.

## SECOND TIE END

**Row 1:** With **right** side facing and working in end of rows across opposite end of Body, join Lavender with slip st in first row; ch 2, work 5{7} dc evenly spaced across: 5{7} dc.

Complete same as First Tie End.

# FLOWER

**Rnd 1** (Right side)**:** With Variegated, ch 2, 6 sc in second ch from hook; join with slip st to first sc.

*Note:* Mark Rnd 1 as **right** side.

**Rnd 2:** Ch 1, turn; sc in same st, ch 1, (sc in next sc, ch 1) around; join with slip st to first sc: 6 ch-1 sps.

**Rnd 3:** (Slip st, ch 1, sc) in next ch-1 sp, ch 2, skip next sc, ★ sc in next ch-1 sp, ch 2, skip next sc; repeat from ★ around; join with slip st to first sc, finish off: 6 ch-2 sps.

**Rnd 4:** With **right** side facing, join Lavender with slip st in any ch-2 sp; (ch 2, 3 dc, ch 2, slip st) in same sp, (slip st, ch 2, 3 dc, ch 2, slip st) in next ch-2 sp and in each ch-2 sp around; join with slip st to first slip st, finish off: 6 petals.

**Rnd 5:** With **right** side facing and working **behind** petals, join Purple with sc in any skipped sc on Rnd 3 *(see Joining With Sc, page 46)*; ch 5, (sc in next sc, ch 5) around; join with slip st to first sc: 6 ch-5 sps.

**Rnd 6:** Ch 1, (sc, ch 2, 5 dc, ch 2, sc) in first ch-5 sp and in each ch-5 sp around; join with slip st to first sc, finish off.

Using photo as a guide for placement, sew Flower to Body.

# BEAUTIFUL BOWS

 **EASY**

**Approximate Finished Measurement (excluding tie)**
3½" wide x 13" long
(9 cm x 33 cm)

## SHOPPING LIST

### Yarn (Medium Weight)
[5 ounces, 244 yards
(141 grams, 233 meters) per skein]:
☐ Variegated - One skein
[7 ounces, 364 yards
(198 grams, 333 meters) per skein]:
☐ Pink - One skein

### Crochet Hook
☐ Size H (5 mm)
**or** size needed for gauge

### Additional Supplies
☐ Yarn needle

## GAUGE INFORMATION

16 sc and 26 rows = 4" (10 cm)
**Gauge Swatch:** 4" (10 cm) square
With Variegated, ch 17.
**Row 1:** Sc in second ch from hook
and in each ch across: 16 sc.
**Rows 2-16:** Ch 1, turn; sc in each sc
across.
Finish off.

## INSTRUCTIONS
### BODY
**Row 1** (Right side)**:** With Variegated,
ch 19, 2 hdc in third ch from hook,
leave remaining 16 chs unworked for
first tie.

*Note:* Loop a short piece of yarn
around any stitch to mark Row 1 as
**right** side.

**Row 2:** Ch 2 (**counts as first hdc,
now and throughout**), turn; hdc in
same st, hdc in next hdc and in next
ch: 4 hdc.

**Rows 3-5:** Ch 2, turn; hdc in same st, hdc in next hdc and in each hdc across: 7 hdc.

**Row 6:** Ch 1, turn; sc in each hdc across.

**Row 7:** Ch 1, turn; 2 sc in first sc, ch 6, skip next 5 sc, 2 sc in last sc: 4 sc and one ch-6 sp.

**Rows 8 and 9:** Ch 1, turn; sc in first 2 sc, ch 6, skip next ch-6 sp, sc in last 2 sc.

**Row 10:** Ch 1, turn; sc in first sc, 2 sc in next sc, ch 2, working **around** previous 2 rows *(Fig. 3, page 46)*, sc in ch-6 sp 3 rows **below**, ch 2, 2 sc in next sc, sc in last sc: 7 sc and 2 ch-2 sps.

**Row 11:** Ch 1, turn; sc in first 3 sc, ch 6, skip next 2 ch-2 sps, sc in last 3 sc: 6 sc and one ch-6 sp.

**Row 12:** Ch 1, turn; sc in first 3 sc, ch 6, skip next ch-6 sp, sc in last 3 sc.

**Row 13:** Ch 1, turn; sc in first sc, 2 sc in next sc, sc in next sc, ch 6, skip next ch-6 sp, sc in next sc, 2 sc in next sc, sc in last sc: 8 sc and one ch-6 sp.

**Row 14:** Ch 1, turn; sc in first 4 sc, ch 2, working **around** previous 2 rows, sc in ch-6 sp 3 rows **below**, ch 2, sc in last 4 sc: 9 sc and 2 ch-2 sps.

**Row 15:** Ch 1, turn; sc in first 4 sc, ch 6, skip next 2 ch-2 sps, sc in last 4 sc: 8 sc and one ch-6 sp.

**Rows 16 and 17:** Ch 1, turn; sc in first 4 sc, ch 6, skip next ch-6 sp, sc in last 4 sc.

**Rows 18-30:** Repeat Rows 14-17, 3 times; then repeat Row 14 once **more**: 9 sc and 2 ch-2 sps.

**Row 31:** Ch 1, turn; skip first sc, sc in next 3 sc, ch 6, skip next 2 ch-2 sps, sc in next 3 sc, slip st in last sc: 6 sc, one slip st, and one ch-6 sp.

**Row 32:** Ch 1, turn; skip first slip st, sc in next 3 sc, ch 6, skip next ch-6 sp, sc in last 3 sc: 6 sc and one ch-6 sp.

**Row 33:** Ch 1, turn; sc in first 3 sc, ch 6, skip next ch-6 sp, sc in last 3 sc.

**Row 34:** Ch 1, turn; sc in first 3 sc, ch 2, working **around** previous 2 rows, sc in ch-6 sp 3 rows **below**, ch 2, sc in last 3 sc: 7 sc and 2 ch-2 sps.

**Row 35:** Ch 1, turn; skip first sc, sc in next 2 sc, ch 6, skip next 2 ch-2 sps, sc in next 2 sc, slip st in last sc: 4 sc, one slip st, and one ch-6 sp.

**Row 36:** Ch 1, turn; skip first slip st, sc in next 2 sc, ch 6, skip next ch-6 sp, sc in last 2 sc: 4 sc and one ch-6 sp.

**Row 37:** Ch 1, turn; sc in first 2 sc, ch 6, skip next ch-6 sp, sc in last 2 sc.

**Row 38:** Ch 1, turn; sc in first 2 sc, ch 2, working **around** previous 2 rows, sc in ch-6 sp 3 rows **below**, ch 2, sc in last 2 sc: 5 sc and 2 ch-2 sps.

**Row 39:** Ch 1, turn; sc in first 2 sc, ch 5, skip next 2 ch-2 sps, sc in last 2 sc: 4 sc and one ch-5 sp.

**Row 40:** Ch 1, turn; skip first sc, sc in next sc, 5 sc in next ch-5 sp, sc in next sc, slip st in last sc: 7 sc and one slip st.

**Row 41:** Ch 2, turn; skip first slip st and next sc, hdc in next sc and in each sc across: 7 hdc.

**Rows 42-44:** Ch 2, turn; hdc in next hdc and in each hdc across to last hdc, leave last hdc unworked: 3 hdc.

**Row 45:** Ch 2, turn; skip first hdc, ★ YO, insert hook in **next** hdc, YO and pull up a loop; repeat from ★ once **more**, YO and draw through all 5 loops on hook; ch 16 for second tie, finish off.

## BOW

### LOOP

With Pink, ch 22.

**Row 1:** Sc in second ch from hook and in each ch across: 21 sc.

**Row 2** (Right side)**:** Ch 1, turn; sc in each sc across.

*Note:* Mark Row 2 as **right** side.

**Row 3:** Ch 1, turn; sc in each sc across; finish off, leaving a long end for sewing.

Thread yarn needle with long end. With **right** side facing and being careful **not** to twist piece, sew ends of rows together.

### TIE

With Pink, ch 7.

**Row 1:** Sc in second ch from hook and in each ch across: 6 sc.

**Row 2:** Ch 1, turn; sc in each sc across; do **not** finish off.

**First Curly-Q:** Ch 12, 3 sc in second ch from hook and in each ch across to last ch, sc in last ch and in top of first sc on Row 1; do **not** finish off.

**Second Curly-Q:** Ch 12, 3 sc in second ch from hook and in each ch across to last ch, sc in last ch; slip st in ch at base of first sc on Row 1; finish off.

Fold Loop in half with seam at center back. Wrap Tie tightly around center of Loop. Sew in place on back side of Loop, allowing Curly-Q's to hang down.

Using photo as a guide for placement and Pink yarn, sew Bow to Body.

# ONE PERFECT ROSE

*Shown on page 25.*

 **EASY**

## SHOPPING LIST

### Yarn (Medium Weight)

[7 ounces, 364 yards
(198 grams, 333 meters) per skein]:

☐ Rose - One skein

☐ Pink - 7 yards (6.5 meters)

☐ Green - Small amount

### Crochet Hooks

☐ Size H (5 mm) **and**

☐ Size I (5.5 mm)

   **or** sizes needed for gauge

### Additional Supplies

☐ Yarn needle

## SIZE INFORMATION

**Approximate Finished**
**Measurement (excluding tie)**

Girl's    3½" wide x 14½" long
          (9 cm x 37 cm)

Teen's    4½" wide x 17" long
          (11.5 cm x 43 cm)

*Size Note:* We have printed the instructions for the sizes in different colors to make it easier for you to find:

• Girl's size in Blue

• Teen's size in Pink

Instructions in Black apply to both sizes.

## GAUGE INFORMATION

With larger size hook, in pattern,
    14 sts = 4" (10 cm)

**Gauge Swatch:** 4" (10 cm) square
With larger size hook and Rose,
ch 15.

**Row 1:** Sc in second ch from hook and in each ch across: 14 sc.

**Rows 1-14:** Ch 1, turn; sc in each sc across.

Finish off.

**TREBLE CROCHET** *(abbreviated tr)*

YO twice, insert hook in st indicated, YO and pull up a loop (4 loops on hook), (YO and draw through 2 loops on hook) 3 times.

**SINGLE CROCHET 2 TOGETHER**
*(abbreviated sc2tog)*

Pull up a loop in each of next 2 sts, YO and draw through all 3 loops on hook (**counts as one sc**).

## INSTRUCTIONS
### BODY

With larger size hook and Rose, ch 40{48}.

**Row 1** (Right side): Working in back ridges of beginning ch *(Fig. 1, page 46)*, sc in second ch from hook and in next 6{7} chs, hdc in next 25{31} chs, sc in last 7{8} chs: 39{47} sts.

*Note:* Loop a short piece of yarn around any stitch to mark Row 1 as **right** side.

**Row 2:** Ch 1, turn; sc in first 2{3} sc, (ch 1, skip next sc, sc in next sc) twice, ch 1, skip next sc, hdc in next hdc, (ch 1, skip next hdc, hdc in next hdc) 3{4} times, (ch 1, skip next hdc, dc in next hdc) 5{6} times, (ch 1, skip next hdc, hdc in next hdc) 4{5} times, ch 1, skip next sc, (sc in next sc, ch 1, skip next sc) twice, sc in last 2{3} sc: 21{26} sts and 18{21} ch-1 sps.

**Row 3:** Ch 1, turn; sc in first 2{3} sc and in next ch-1 sp, (ch 1, skip next sc, sc in next ch-1 sp) twice, (ch 1, skip next hdc, hdc in next ch-1 sp) 3{4} times, ch 1, skip next hdc, dc in next ch-1 sp, (ch 1, skip next dc, dc in next ch-1 sp) 5{6} times, ch 1, skip next dc, hdc in next ch-1 sp, (ch 1, skip next hdc, hdc in next ch-1 sp) 2{3} times, (ch 1, skip next st, sc in next ch-1 sp) 3 times, sc in last 2{3} sc: 22{27} sts and 17{20} ch-1 sps.

**Row 4:** Ch 1, turn; sc in first 2{3} sc, (ch 1, skip next sc, sc in next ch-1 sp) twice, ch 1, skip next sc, hdc in next ch-1 sp, (ch 1, skip next hdc, hdc in next ch-1 sp) 3{4} times, (ch 1, skip next dc, dc in next ch-1 sp) 5{6} times, ch 1, skip next dc, hdc in next ch-1 sp, (ch 1, skip next hdc, hdc in next ch-1 sp) 3{4} times, ch 1, (skip next sc, sc in next ch-1 sp, ch 1) twice, skip next sc, sc in last 2{3} sc: 21{26} sts and 18{21} ch-1 sps.

**Rows 5 thru 6{8}:** Repeat Rows 3 and 4, 1{2} time(s): 21{26} sts and 18{21} ch-1 sps.

**Row 7{9}:** Ch 1, turn; sc in first 2{3} sc and in next ch-1 sp, (sc in next sc and in next ch-1 sp) twice, (hdc in next st and in next ch-1 sp) 12{15} times, hdc in next hdc, sc in next ch-1 sp, (sc in next sc and in next ch-1 sp) twice, sc in last 2{3} sc; do **not** finish off: 39{47} sts.

**FIRST TIE END**
**Row 1:** Ch 1, do **not** turn; work 5{6} sc evenly spaced across end of rows.

**Row 2:** Ch 1, turn; skip first sc, sc in last 4{5} sc: 4{5} sc.

**Row 3:** Ch 1, turn; skip first sc, sc in last 3{4} sc: 3{4} sc.

**Teen's Size ONLY**
**Row 4:** Ch 1, turn; skip first sc, sc in last 3 sc: 3 sc.

**Both Sizes**
**Last Row:** Ch 1, turn; skip first sc, sc2tog, ch 18 for tie; finish off.

## SECOND TIE END

**Row 1:** With **right** side facing, using larger size hook, and working in ends of rows across opposite end of Body, join Rose with sc in first row *(see Joining With Sc, page 46)*; work 4{5} sc evenly spaced across: 5{6} sc.

Complete same as First Tie End.

## FLOWER

With smaller size hook and Rose, ch 30.

**Row 1:** Sc in second ch from hook, ch 2, skip next ch, sc in next ch, ch 2, skip next ch, sc in next 5 chs, ch 2, skip next ch, sc in next 3 chs, (ch 2, skip next ch, sc in next ch) across: 18 sc and 11 ch-2 sps.

**Row 2** (Right side)**:** Turn; slip st in first sc, (slip st, ch 1, 3 hdc, ch 1, slip st) in each of next 3 ch-2 sps, slip st in next ch-2 sp changing to Pink *(Fig. A)*, cut Rose; (ch 2, 4 dc, ch 2, slip st) in same sp, (slip st, ch 2, 4 dc, ch 2, slip st) in each of next 4 ch-2 sps, slip st in next 3 sc, slip st in next ch-2 sp changing to Green, cut Pink; **[**ch 6, slip st in second ch from hook, hdc in next ch, dc in next ch, tr in next ch, dc in next ch **(leaf made)]**, slip st in same ch-2 sp and in next 5 sc, (work leaf, slip st in next sc) twice; finish off.

**Fig. A**

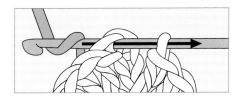

Thread yarn needle with a 10" (25.5 cm) length of Rose. Using photo as a guide, roll Flower with **right** side facing, spacing petals evenly. Tack petals in place on **wrong** side of Flower, then sew to Body.

# SO SERENE

 **EASY**

## SHOPPING LIST

**Yarn** (Medium Weight)

[7 ounces, 364 yards
(198 grams, 333 meters) per skein]:

☐ Grey - One skein

☐ Variegated - 8 yards
(7.5 meters)

☐ White - Small amount

## Crochet Hooks

☐ Size I (5.5 mm) **and**

☐ Size K (6.5 mm)

**or** sizes needed for gauge

## Additional Supplies

☐ Yarn needle

## SIZE INFORMATION

**Approximate Finished
Measurement (excluding tie)**

Girl's   3¼" wide x 15" long
(8.5 cm x 38 cm)

Teen's   4¼" wide x 18" long
(10.75 cm x 45.5 cm)

*Size Note:* We have printed the instructions for the sizes in different colors to make it easier for you to find:

• Girl's size in Blue

• Teen's size in Pink

Instructions in Black apply to both sizes.

## GAUGE INFORMATION

With larger size hook, in pattern,
12 sts = 4" (10 cm)

**Gauge Swatch:** 4" wide x 4¼" high
(10 cm x 10.75 cm)

With larger size hook and Grey, ch 14.

**Row 1:** Dc in fourth ch from hook **(3 skipped chs count as first dc)** and in each ch across: 12 dc.

**Row 2:** Ch 3 **(counts as first dc, now and throughout)**, turn; work FPdc around next dc, (dc in next dc, work FPdc around next dc) across.

**Row 3:** Ch 3, turn; dc in next dc and in each st across.

**Rows 4-8:** Repeat Rows 2 and 3 twice, then repeat Row 2 once **more**. Finish off.

# STITCH GUIDE

**TREBLE CROCHET** *(abbreviated tr)*
YO twice, insert hook in st or sp indicated, YO and pull up a loop (4 loops on hook), (YO and draw through 2 loops on hook) 3 times.
**FRONT POST DOUBLE CROCHET**
    *(abbreviated FPdc)*
YO, insert hook from **front** to **back** around post of st indicated *(Fig. 2, page 46)*, YO and pull up a loop (3 loops on hook), (YO and draw through 2 loops on hook) twice.

---

# INSTRUCTIONS
## BODY

With larger size hook and Grey, ch 40{48}.

**Row 1** (Right side)**:** Sc in second ch from hook and in next 4{5} chs, hdc in next 9{11} chs, dc in next 11(13) chs, hdc in next 9{11} chs, sc in last 5{6} chs: 39{47} sts.

*Note:* Loop a short piece of yarn around any stitch to mark Row 1 as **right** side.

**Row 2:** Ch 1, turn; sc in first 5{6} sc, work FPdc around next st, (dc in next st, work FPdc around next st) 14{17} times, sc in last 5{6} sc.

**Row 3:** Ch 1, turn; sc in first 5{6} sc, hdc in next 9{11} sts, dc in next 11{13} sts, hdc in next 9{11} sts, sc in last 5{6} sc.

**Rows 4 thru 6{8}:** Repeat Rows 2 and 3, 1{2} time(s), then repeat Row 2 once **more**.

Do **not** finish off.

## FIRST TIE END
**Row 1:** Ch 1, do **not** turn; work 5{6} sc evenly spaced across end of rows.

**Row 2:** Ch 1, turn; skip first sc, sc in next 3{4} sc, slip st in last sc: 3{4} sc and one slip st.

**Row 3:** Ch 1, turn; skip first slip st, sc in next 2{3} sc, slip st in last sc: 2{3} sc and one slip st.

**Teen's Size ONLY**
**Row 4:** Ch 1, turn; skip first slip st, sc in next 2 sc, slip st in last sc: 2 sc and one slip st.

**Both Sizes**
**Last Row:** Ch 1, turn; skip first slip st, pull up a loop in each of next 2 sc, YO and draw through all 3 loops on hook, ch 16 for tie; finish off.

## SECOND TIE END
**Row 1:** With **wrong** side facing, using larger size hook and working in end of rows across opposite end of Body, join Grey with sc in first row *(see Joining With Sc, page 46)*; work 4{5} sc evenly spaced across: 5{6} sc.

Complete same as First Tie End.

# FLOWER
**Rnd 1** (Right side)**:** With smaller size hook and White, ch 2, 6 sc in second ch from hook; do **not** join, place a marker to mark the beginning of the rnd *(see Markers, page 45)*.

*Note:* Mark Rnd 1 as **right** side.

**Rnd 2:** 2 Sc in each sc around; slip st in next sc, finish off: 12 sts.

**Rnd 3:** With **right** side facing and using smaller size hook, join Variegated with slip st in any sc; (dc, tr) in same st, (tr, dc, slip st) in next sc, ★ (slip st, dc, tr) in next sc, (tr, dc, slip st) in next sc; repeat from ★ around; do **not** join, place a marker to mark the beginning of the rnd: 6 petals.

**Rnd 4:** Working **behind** petals, ★ ch 5, skip next petal and next slip st, slip st in next slip st; repeat from ★ working last slip st at base of first ch-5: 6 ch-5 sps.

**Rnd 5:** (Slip st, sc, dc, 3 tr, dc, sc, slip st) in each ch-5 sp around; join with slip st to first slip st, finish off.

Using photo as a guide for placement, sew Flower to Body.

# OH, THE FRILL

 **EASY**

## SHOPPING LIST

**Yarn** (Medium Weight)
[6 ounces, 315 yards
(170 grams, 288 meters) per skein]:
☐ Blue - One skein
☐ White - Small amount

## Crochet Hook
☐ Size I (5.5 mm)
**or** size needed for gauge

## Additional Supplies
☐ Yarn needle

## SIZE INFORMATION
**Approximate Finished
Measurement (excluding tie)**

Girl's     4" wide x 14" long
            (10 cm x 35.5 cm)
Teen's    4¾" wide x 17¼" long
            (12 cm x 44 cm)

*Size Note:* We have printed the instructions for the sizes in different colors to make it easier for you to find:
• Girl's size in Blue
• Teen's size in Pink
Instructions in Black apply to both sizes.

## GAUGE INFORMATION
In pattern, 13 sts = 4" (10 cm)
**Gauge Swatch:** 4" (10 cm) square
With Blue, ch 14.
**Row 1:** Sc in second ch from hook and in each ch across: 13 sc.
**Rows 2-13:** Ch 1, turn; sc in each sc across.
Finish off.

## —— STITCH GUIDE ——

**PUFF ST** (uses one st)

★ YO, insert hook in st indicated, YO and pull up a loop even with loops on hook; repeat from ★ 3 times **more**, YO and draw through all 9 loops on hook, ch 1 to close.

**SINGLE CROCHET 2 TOGETHER**

(abbreviated sc2tog)

Pull up a loop in each of next 2 sts, YO and draw through all 3 loops on hook (**counts as one sc**).

# INSTRUCTIONS
## BODY

With Blue, ch 40{48}.

**Row 1:** Working in back ridges of beginning ch (**Fig. 1, page 46**), sc in second ch from hook and in next 4 chs, hdc in next 10{12} chs, dc in next 9{13} chs, hdc in next 10{12} chs, sc in last 5 chs: 39{47} sts.

**Row 2** (Right side)**:** Ch 1, turn; sc in first 5 sc, work Puff St in next hdc, ★ ch 1, skip next st, dc in next st, ch 1, skip next st, work Puff St in next st; repeat from ★ across to last 5 sc, sc in last 5 sc: 8{10} Puff Sts and 14{18} ch-1 sps.

*Note:* Loop a short piece of yarn around any stitch to mark Row 2 as **right** side.

**Row 3:** Ch 1, turn; sc in first 5 sc, (skip next st, 2 hdc in next ch-1 sp) 5{6} times, (skip next st, 2 dc in next ch-1 sp) 4{6} times, (skip next st, 2 hdc in next ch-1 sp) 5{6} times, hdc in next Puff St, sc in last 5 sc: 39{47} sts.

**Rows 4 thru 7{9}:** Repeat Rows 2 and 3, 2{3} times.

Do **not** finish off.

**FIRST TIE END**
**Row 1:** Ch 1, do **not** turn; work 5{7} sc evenly spaced across end of rows: 5{7} sc.

**Row 2:** Ch 1, turn; skip first sc, sc in last 4{6} sc: 4{6} sc.

**Row 3:** Ch 1, turn; skip first sc, sc in last 3{5} sc: 3{5} sc.

**Row 4:** Ch 1, turn; skip first sc, sc in last 2{4} sc: 2{4} sc.

**Teen's Size ONLY**

**Row 5:** Ch 1, turn; skip first sc, sc in last 3 sc: 3 sc.

**Row 6:** Ch 1, turn; skip first sc, sc in last 2 sc: 2 sc.

**Both Sizes**

**Last Row:** Ch 1, turn; sc2tog, ch 16 for tie; finish off.

**SECOND TIE END**

**Row 1:** With **wrong** side facing and working in end of rows across opposite end of Body, join Blue with sc in first row *(see Joining With Sc, page 46)*; work 4{6} sc evenly spaced across: 5{7} sc.

Complete same as First Tie End.

## FLOWER

**Rnd 1** (Right side)**:** With White, ch 2, 5 sc in second ch from hook; join with slip st to first sc.

*Note:* Mark Rnd 1 as **right** side.

**Rnd 2:** Ch 1, 2 sc in same st and in each sc around; join with slip st to first sc, finish off: 10 sc.

**Rnd 3:** With **wrong** side facing, join Blue with slip st in any sc; (ch 2, work Puff St, ch 2, slip st) in same st, (slip st, ch 2, work Puff St, ch 2, slip st) in next sc and in each sc around; join with slip st to first slip st, finish off: 10 Puff Sts and 20 ch-2 sps.

**Rnd 4:** With **right** side facing, join White with sc in first ch-2 sp; ch 3, skip next Puff St and next ch-2 sp, ★ sc in next ch-2 sp, ch 3, skip next Puff St and next ch-2 sp; repeat from ★ around; join with slip st to first sc, finish off.

Using photo as a guide for placement, sew Flower to Body.

# SIMPLY FUN

 **EASY**

## SIZE INFORMATION

**Approximate Finished
Measurement (excluding tie)**

Girl's      3½" wide x 15" long
            (9 cm x 38 cm)

Teen's      4¾" wide x 19" long
            (12 cm x 48.5 cm)

*Size Note:* We have printed the instructions for the sizes in different colors to make it easier for you to find:

• Girl's size in Blue

• Teen's size in Pink

Instructions in Black apply to both sizes.

## GAUGE INFORMATION

Dc, (ch 3, dc) twice = 2½" (6.25 cm)

**Gauge Swatch:** 2½" (6.25 cm) square

With Pink, ch 14.

**Row 1:** Dc in tenth ch from hook **(first 6 skipped chs count as first dc plus ch 3)**, ch 3, skip next 3 chs, dc in last ch: 3 dc and 2 ch-2 sps.

**Rows 2-4:** Ch 6 **(counts as first dc plus ch 3)**, turn; dc in next dc, ch 3, skip next ch-3 sp, dc in last dc. Finish off.

# INSTRUCTIONS
## BODY

With Pink, ch 50{62}.

**Row 1:** Sc in second ch from hook, ch 3, skip next 3 chs, sc in next ch, (ch 3, skip next 3 chs, hdc in next ch) 3{4} times, (ch 3, skip next 3 chs, dc in next ch) 3{4} times, (ch 3, skip next 3 chs, hdc in next ch) 3{4} times, (ch 3, skip next 3 chs, sc in next ch) twice: 13{16} sts and 12{15} ch-3 sps.

**Row 2** (Right side)**:** Ch 1, turn; sc in first sc, ch 3, skip next ch-3 sp, sc in next sc, (ch 3, skip next ch-3 sp, hdc in next hdc) 3{4} times, (ch 3, skip next ch-3 sp, dc in next dc) 3{4} times, (ch 3, skip next ch-3 sp, hdc in next hdc) 3{4} times, (ch 3, skip next ch-3 sp, sc in next sc) twice.

*Note:* Loop a short piece of yarn around any stitch to mark Row 2 as **right** side.

**Rows 3 thru 6{8}:** Ch 1, turn; sc in first sc, ch 3, skip next ch-3 sp, sc in next sc, (ch 3, skip next ch-3 sp, hdc in next hdc) 3{4} times, (ch 3, skip next ch-3 sp, dc in next dc) 3{4} times, (ch 3, skip next ch-3 sp, hdc in next hdc) 3{4} times, (ch 3, skip next ch-3 sp, sc in next sc) twice.

Do **not** finish off.

**FIRST TIE END**

**Row 1:** Ch 1, do **not** turn; working in end of rows, work 5{7} sc evenly spaced across: 5{7} sc.

**Row 2:** Ch 1, turn; skip first sc, sc in last 4{6} sc: 4{6} sc.

**Row 3:** Ch 1, turn; skip first sc, sc in last 3{5} sc: 3{5} sc.

**Row 4:** Ch 1, turn; skip first sc, sc in last 2{4} sc: 2{4} sc.

**Teen's Size ONLY**

**Row 5:** Ch 1, turn; skip first sc, sc in last 3 sc: 3 sc.

**Row 6:** Ch 1, turn; skip first sc, sc in last 2 sc: 2 sc.

**Both Sizes**
**Last Row:** Ch 1, turn; skip first sc, sc in last sc, ch 16 for tie; finish off.

### SECOND TIE END
**Row 1:** With **right** side facing and working in end of rows across opposite end of Body, join Pink with sc in first row *(see Joining With Sc, page 46)*; work 4{6} sc evenly spaced across: 5{7} sc.

Complete same as First Tie End.

## FLOWER
With White, ch 4; join with slip st to form a ring.

**Rnd 1** (Right side)**:** Ch 2 (**counts as first hdc**), 11 hdc in ring; join with slip st to first hdc, finish off: 12 hdc.

*Note:* Mark Rnd 1 as **right** side.

**Rnd 2:** With **right** side facing, join Pink with sc in any hdc; ch 3, skip next hdc, ★ sc in next hdc, ch 3, skip next hdc; repeat from ★ around; join with slip st to first sc: 6 ch-3 sps.

**Rnd 3:** (Slip st, 2 hdc, dc, 2 hdc, slip st) in first ch-3 sp and in each ch-3 sp around; join with slip st to first slip st, finish off: 6 petals.

**Rnd 4:** With **right** side facing and working **behind** petals, join Green with sc in any skipped hdc on Rnd 1; ch 5, (sc in next skipped hdc, ch 5) around; join with slip st to first sc: 6 ch-5 sps.

**Rnd 5:** Ch 1, (sc, 2 hdc, 2 dc, 2 hdc, sc) in first ch-5 sp and in each ch-5 sp around; join with slip st to first sc, finish off.

Using photo as a guide for placement, sew Flower to Body.

# OUT OF THE BLUE

## SHOPPING LIST

**Yarn** (Medium Weight)

[6 ounces, 315 yards
(170 grams, 288 meters) per skein]:

☐ Blue - One skein

☐ Dk Blue - 10 yards (9.5 meters)

☐ Green - 7 yards (6.5 meters)

☐ White - Small amount

## Crochet Hooks

☐ Size G (4 mm) **and**

☐ Size I (5.5 mm)

**or** sizes needed for gauge

## Additional Supplies

☐ Yarn needle

## SIZE INFORMATION

**Approximate Finished
Measurement (excluding tie)**

Girl's      4" wide x 15" long
(10 cm x 38 cm)

Teen's    4¾" wide x 18¾" long
(12 cm x 47.5 cm)

*Size Note:* We have printed the
instructions for the sizes in different
colors to make it easier for you to
find:

• Girl's size in Blue

• Teen's size in Pink

Instructions in Black apply to both
sizes.

## GAUGE INFORMATION

With larger size hook,
15 sts = 4" (10 cm)

**Gauge Swatch:** 4" (10 cm) square

With larger size hook and Blue, ch 16.

**Row 1:** Sc in second ch from hook
and in each ch across: 15 sc.

**Rows 2-15:** Ch 1, turn; sc in each sc
across.

Finish off.

## STITCH GUIDE

**FRONT POST
DOUBLE CROCHET**

*(abbreviated FPdc)*

YO, insert hook from **front** to **back** around post of st indicated *(Fig. 2, page 46)*, YO and pull up a loop (3 loops on hook), (YO and draw through 2 loops on hook) twice.

**SINGLE CROCHET 2 TOGETHER**

*(abbreviated sc2tog)*

Pull up a loop in each of next 2 sts, YO and draw through all 3 loops on hook **(counts as one sc).**

# INSTRUCTIONS
## BODY

With larger size hook and Blue,
ch 49{58}.

**Row 1:** Working in back ridges of
beginning ch *(Fig. 1, page 46)*, sc in
second ch from hook and in each ch
across: 48{57} sc.

**Row 2** (Right side)**:** Ch 1, turn; sc
in first 3 sc, skip next sc, [(sc, ch 1,
sc) in next sc, skip next 2 sc] twice,
[(hdc, ch 1, hdc) in next sc, skip next
2 sc] 3{4} times, [(dc, ch 1, dc) in
next sc, skip next 2 sc] 4{5} times,
[(hdc, ch 1, hdc) in next sc, skip next
2 sc] 3{4} times, (sc, ch 1, sc) in next
sc, skip next 2 sc, (sc, ch 1, sc) in
next sc, skip next sc, sc in last 3 sc:
34{40} sts and 14{17} ch-1 sps.

*Note:* Loop a short piece of yarn
around any stitch to mark Row 2 as
**right** side.

**Rows 3 thru 8{10}:** Ch 1, turn; sc in
first 3 sc, skip next sc, [(sc, ch 1, sc)
in next ch-1 sp, skip next 2 sts] twice,
[(hdc, ch 1, hdc) in next ch-1 sp, skip
next 2 sts] 3{4} times, [(dc, ch 1, dc)
in next ch-1 sp, skip next 2 sts] 4{5}
times, [(hdc, ch 1, hdc) in next
ch-1 sp, skip next 2 sts] 3{4} times,
(sc, ch 1, sc) in next ch-1 sp, skip next
2 sc, (sc, ch 1, sc) in next ch-1 sp, skip
next sc, sc in last 3 sc.

**Row 9{11}:** Ch 1, turn; slip st in first
sc, sc in next 3 sc, 2 sc in next ch-1 sp,
★ sc in sp **before** next st *(Fig. 4,
page 46)*, skip next st, 2 sc in next
ch-1 sp; repeat from ★ across to last
4 sc, sc in next 3 sc, slip st in last sc;
do **not** finish off: 49{58} sts.

### FIRST TIE END
**Row 1:** Ch 1, do **not** turn; work
6{7} sc evenly spaced across end of
rows: 6{7} sc.

**Row 2:** Ch 1, turn; skip first sc, sc in
next 4{5} sc, slip st in last sc: 4{5} sc.

**Girl's Size ONLY**

**Row 3:** Ch 1, turn; skip first sc, sc in last 3 sc: 3 sc.

**Teen's Size ONLY**

**Row 3:** Ch 1, turn; skip first sc, sc in next 3 sc, slip st in last sc: 3 sc.

**Both Sizes**

**Row 4:** Ch 1, turn; skip first sc, sc2tog, ch 18 for tie; finish off.

**SECOND TIE END**

**Row 1:** With **wrong** side facing, using larger size hook, and working in end of rows across opposite end of Body, join Blue with sc in first row *(see Joining With Sc, page 46)*; work 5{6} sc evenly spaced across: 6{7} sc.

Complete same as First Tie End.

# FLOWER

**Rnd 1** (Right side)**:** With smaller size hook and White, ch 4, 11 dc in fourth ch from hook; join with slip st to top of beginning ch, finish off: 12 sts.

*Note:* Mark Rnd 1 as **right** side.

**Rnd 2:** With **right** side facing, join Blue with slip st in same st as joining; ch 3 (**counts as first dc, now and throughout**), work FPdc around same st, (dc in next dc, work FPdc around same st) around; join with slip st to first dc, finish off: 24 sts.

**Rnd 3:** With **right** side facing, skip first dc and join Green with slip st in next FPdc; ch 4 (**counts as first dc plus ch 1**), dc in same st, skip next dc, ★ (dc, ch 1, dc) in next FPdc, skip next dc; repeat from ★ around; join with slip st to first dc, finish off: 24 dc and 12 ch-1 sps.

**Rnd 4:** With **right** side facing, join Dk Blue with slip st in first ch-1 sp; ch 3, 6 dc in same sp, slip st in next ch-1 sp, (7 dc in next ch-1 sp, slip st in next ch-1 sp) around; join with slip st to first dc, finish off.

Using photo as a guide for placement, sew Flower to Body.

# GENERAL INSTRUCTIONS

## ABBREVIATIONS

| | |
|---|---|
| ch(s) | chain(s) |
| cm | centimeters |
| dc | double crochet(s) |
| FPdc | Front Post double crochet(s) |
| hdc | half double crochet(s) |
| mm | millimeters |
| Rnd(s) | Round(s) |
| sc | single crochet(s) |
| sc2tog | single crochet 2 together |
| sp(s) | space(s) |
| st(s) | stitch(es) |
| tr | treble crochet(s) |
| YO | yarn over |

## SYMBOLS & TERMS

★ — work instructions following ★ as many **more** times as indicated in addition to the first time.

( ) or [ ] — work enclosed instructions **as many** times as specified by the number immediately following **or** work all enclosed instructions in the stitch or space indicated **or** contains explanatory remarks.

colon (:) — the number(s) given after a colon at the end of a row or round denote(s) the number of stitches or spaces you should have on that row or round.

| CROCHET HOOKS | | | | | | | | | | | | | | | |
|---|---|---|---|---|---|---|---|---|---|---|---|---|---|---|---|
| U.S. | B-1 | C-2 | D-3 | E-4 | F-5 | G-6 | H-8 | I-9 | J-10 | K-10½ | L-11 | M/N-13 | N/P-15 | P/Q | Q | S |
| Metric - mm | 2.25 | 2.75 | 3.25 | 3.5 | 3.75 | 4 | 5 | 5.5 | 6 | 6.5 | 8 | 9 | 10 | 15 | 16 | 19 |

| | | |
|---|---|---|
| ◼◻◻◻ BEGINNER | Projects for first-time crocheters using basic stitches. Minimal shaping. |
| ◼◼◻◻ EASY | Projects using yarn with basic stitches, repetitive stitch patterns, simple color changes, and simple shaping and finishing. |
| ◼◼◼◻ INTERMEDIATE | Projects using a variety of techniques, such as basic lace patterns or color patterns, mid-level shaping and finishing. |
| ◼◼◼◼ EXPERIENCED | Projects with intricate stitch patterns, techniques and dimension, such as non-repeating patterns, multi-color techniques, fine threads, small hooks, detailed shaping and refined finishing. |

# GAUGE

Exact gauge is **essential** for proper size. Before beginning your project, make the sample swatch given in the individual instructions in the yarn and hook specified. After completing the swatch, measure it, counting your stitches and rows carefully. If your swatch is larger or smaller than specified, **make another, changing hook size to get the correct gauge**. Keep trying until you find the size hook that will give you the specified gauge.

# MARKERS

Markers are used to help distinguish the beginning of each round being worked. Place a 2" (5 cm) scrap piece of yarn before the first stitch of each round, moving marker after each round is complete.

| CROCHET TERMINOLOGY | |
|---|---|
| UNITED STATES | INTERNATIONAL |
| slip stitch (slip st) = | single crochet (sc) |
| single crochet (sc) = | double crochet (dc) |
| half double crochet (hdc) = | half treble crochet (htr) |
| double crochet (dc) = | treble crochet(tr) |
| treble crochet (tr) = | double treble crochet (dtr) |
| double treble crochet (dtr) = | triple treble crochet (ttr) |
| triple treble crochet (tr tr) = | quadruple treble crochet (qtr) |
| skip = | miss |

| Yarn Weight Symbol & Names | LACE 0 | SUPER FINE 1 | FINE 2 | LIGHT 3 | MEDIUM 4 | BULKY 5 | SUPER BULKY 6 |
|---|---|---|---|---|---|---|---|
| Type of Yarns in Category | Fingering, 10-count crochet thread | Sock, Fingering Baby | Sport, Baby | DK, Light Worsted | Worsted, Afghan, Aran | Chunky, Craft, Rug | Bulky, Roving |
| Crochet Gauge* Ranges in Single Crochet to 4" (10 cm) | 32-42 double crochets** | 21-32 sts | 16-20 sts | 12-17 sts | 11-14 sts | 8-11 sts | 5-9 sts |
| Advised Hook Size Range | Steel*** 6,7,8 Regular hook B-1 | B-1 to E-4 | E-4 to 7 | 7 to I-9 | I-9 to K-10.5 | K-10.5 to M-13 | M-13 and larger |

*GUIDELINES ONLY: The chart above reflects the most commonly used gauges and hook sizes for specific yarn categories.

** Lace weight yarns are usually crocheted on larger-size hooks to create lacy openwork patterns. Accordingly, a gauge range is difficult to determine. Always follow the gauge stated in your pattern.

*** Steel crochet hooks are sized differently from regular hooks—the higher the number the smaller the hook, which is the reverse of regular hook sizing.

## JOINING WITH SC

When instructed to join with sc, begin with a slip knot on hook. Insert hook in stitch or space indicated, YO and pull up a loop, YO and draw through both loops on hook.

## BACK RIDGE

Work only in loops indicated by arrows *(Fig. 1)*.

**Fig. 1**

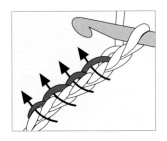

## FRONT POST STITCH

Work around post of stitch indicated, inserting hook in direction of arrow *(Fig. 2)*.

**Fig. 2**

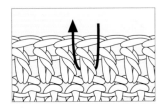

## WORKING AROUND A STITCH

Work in stitch or space indicated, inserting hook in direction of arrow *(Fig. 3)*.

**Fig. 3**

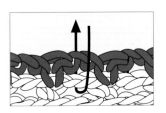

## WORKING IN SPACE BEFORE A STITCH

When instructed to work in space **before** a stitch or in a space **between** stitches, insert hook in space indicated by arrow *(Fig. 4)*.

**Fig. 4**

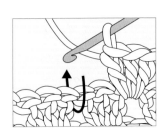

# YARN INFORMATION

Projects in this book were made using Medium Weight Yarn. Any brand of Medium Weight Yarn may be used. It is best to refer to the yardage/meters when determining how many balls or skeins to purchase. Remember, to arrive at the finished size, it is the GAUGE/TENSION that is important, not the brand of yarn.

For your convenience, listed below are the yarns used to create our photography models.

### DAISY DELIGHT
*Red Heart® Super Saver®*
Green - #624 Tea Leaf
White - #311 White
Yellow - #324 Bright Yellow

### SIMPLY ELEGANT
*Red Heart® Super Saver®*
#656 Real Teal

### SO REFINED
*Red Heart® Super Saver®*
#400 Grey Heather

### PETAL POWER
*Caron® Simply Soft®*
Lavender - #9610 Grape
Purple - #9747 Iris
Variegated - information unavailable

### BEAUTIFUL BOWS
*Red Heart® Super Saver®*
Variegated - #929 Bikini
Pink - #722 Pretty 'n Pink

### ONE PERFECT ROSE
*Red Heart® Super Saver®*
Rose - #774 Light Raspberry
Pink - #706 Perfect Pink
Green - #624 Tea Leaf

### SO SERENE
*Red Heart® Super Saver®*
Grey - #400 Grey Heather
Variegated - information unavailable
White - #311 White

### OH, THE FRILL
*Caron® Simply Soft®*
Blue - #9609 Berry Blue
White - #9701 White

### SIMPLY FUN
*Caron® Simply Soft®*
Pink - #9719 Soft Pink
Green - #9739 Soft Green
White - #9701 White

### OUT OF THE BLUE
*Caron® Simply Soft®*
Blue - #9712 Soft Blue
Dk Blue - #9609 Berry Blue
Green - #9739 Soft Green
White - #9701 White

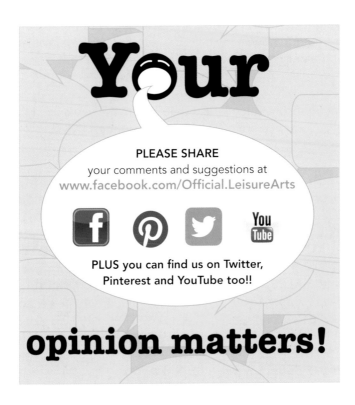

PLEASE SHARE
your comments and suggestions at
www.facebook.com/Official.LeisureArts

PLUS you can find us on Twitter,
Pinterest and YouTube too!!

Production Team: Writer/Technical Editor - Linda A. Daley; Editorial Writer - Susan Frantz Wiles; Senior Graphic Artist - Lora Puls; Graphic Artist - Becca Snider Tally, Dana Vaughn, and Jessica Bramlett; Photo Stylist - Brooke Duszota; and Photographer - Jason Masters.

We have made every effort to ensure that these instructions are accurate and complete. We cannot, however, be responsible for human error, typographical mistakes, or variations in individual work.